DORSET RAMBLES

Ten Country Walks around Dorset

Barry Shurlock

With Historical Notes

COUNTRYSIDE BOOKS
NEWBURY, BERKSHIRE

First Published 1987

Revised Edition 1989

COUNTRYSIDE BOOKS
3 Catherine Road
Newbury, Berkshire
ISBN 0 905392 79 5

Also by Barry Shurlock:
The Solent Way
The Test Way
Hampshire: A Portrait in Colour
Explore Hampshire (with John Holder)

The Cover photograph is a view from the walk on the
Golden Cap Estate

Produced through MRM (Print Consultants) Ltd, Reading
Printed in England by J.W. Arrowsmith Ltd., Bristol

Contents

Introduction		6
Walk 1	CRANBORNE CHASE	9
Walk 2	ST ALDHELM'S HEAD AND THE PURBECK COAST	15
Walk 3	THE NORTH DORSET DOWNS	19
Walk 4	FOLLY AND THE DORSETSHIRE GAP	25
Walk 5	CLOUDS HILL AND T. E. LAWRENCE	29
Walk 6	THOMAS HARDY COUNTRY	35
Walk 7	DURDLE DOOR TO BURNING CLIFF	41
Walk 8	MAIDEN CASTLE	47
Walk 9	CHESIL BEACH AND THE MOHUNS OF FLEET	53
Walk 10	THE GOLDEN CAP ESTATE	59
Further Reading		64

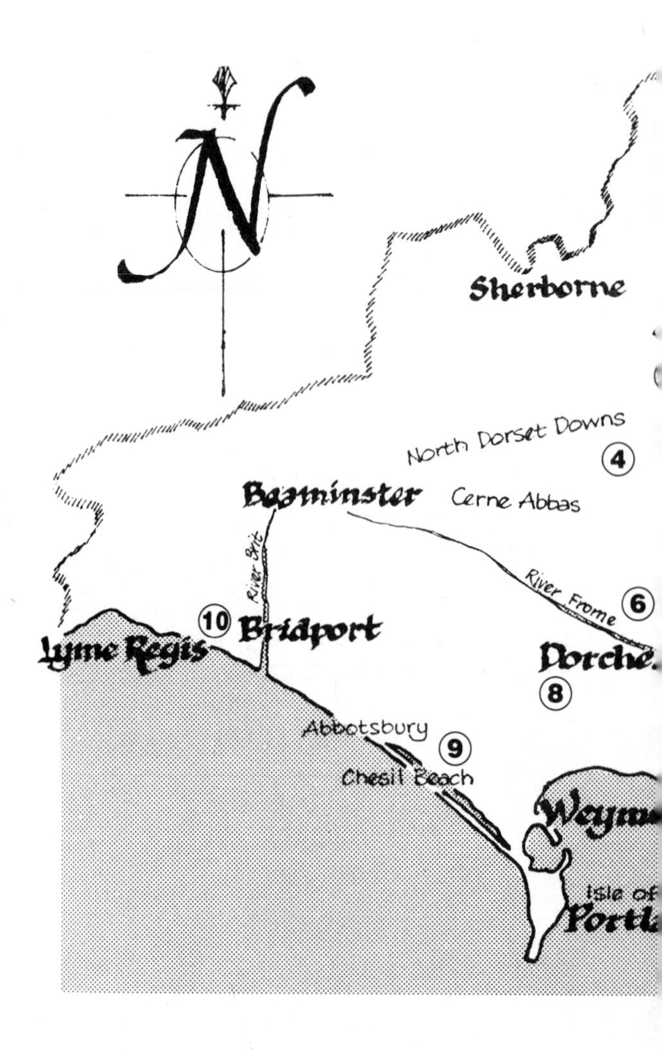

Sherborne
North Dorset Downs
4
Beaminster
Cerne Abbas
River Brit
River Frome
6
10
Bridport
Lyme Regis
8
Abbotsbury
9
Chesil Beach
Isle of

Sketch map showing locations of the walks.

Introduction

Dorset is a walker's paradise. Its hills, its outstanding coastline and the charm of its countryside leave pleasant memories from a stroll almost anywhere in the County. The walks in this book take full advantage of its great variety of scenery. At the same time they are leisurely, enjoyable affairs and should be walkable in an easy morning or afternoon.

One of the problems of preparing a book like this is to know what to put in and what to leave out. I started with a 'short' list of about fifty possible rambles, which with great difficulty I whittled down to a manageable number. The final selection was made on the basis of geographical spread, a determination to include most of the best ones and an element of pot-luck.

All of the rambles follow a circular route. 'How to get there' instructions from major towns are provided with suggested parking spots, most of them designated car parks.

Many people like to combine a walk with a stop-off at a pub or restaurant and most of the walks enable this to be done, as indicated under the 'Refreshments' section of each walk.

Each route is described in detail, probably giving more instructions than are strictly necessary. I have preferred to err on the side of redundancy, even pedantry, to allow for the inevitable changes to routes that will take place – a gate removed, a hedge grubbed out, etc. If the instructions appear not to make sense, assume that such changes have been made and use good old-fashioned commonsense to head off in roughly the right direction.

The sketch map that accompanies each walk is intended as a broad-brush guide to the route. For walkers who like the benefit of more detailed maps three sheets of the 1:50,000 Ordnance Survey (formerly the one-inch series) cover all the rambles.

In the belief that half the joy of a walk is in 'reading' the landscape I have included fairly copious background notes. Where appropriate, these have been woven into the walk instructions, but more often they have been written as separate sections and included at the end of each walk. It is probably best to skip through them before setting out, and then to refer to them as required en route or at home.

The notes are inevitably a personal selection. They have relied heavily on a few standard works, which for the interested reader are listed, together with a number of other books on Dorset, at the end of the book. They tend to be historical, but Dorset is such a rich county for revealing the geological niceties of the countryside (its 'undersoil'?) that I have included a few technical passages where I felt that it would help in understanding the landscape.

Experienced ramblers will not need to be told that a few simple preparations add greatly to the pleasures of walking. Boots or stout shoes and thick socks are virtually essential. Also, depending on the weather, waterproofs and 'one more jumper than you think you'll need' should be carried. Finally, several of the walks are along the top of tall cliffs: please take care.

I am always glad to hear from ramblers who have used the book, and am grateful to those who have made comments and observations.

I hope that you will enjoy these walks as much as I have.

Barry Shurlock
March 1989

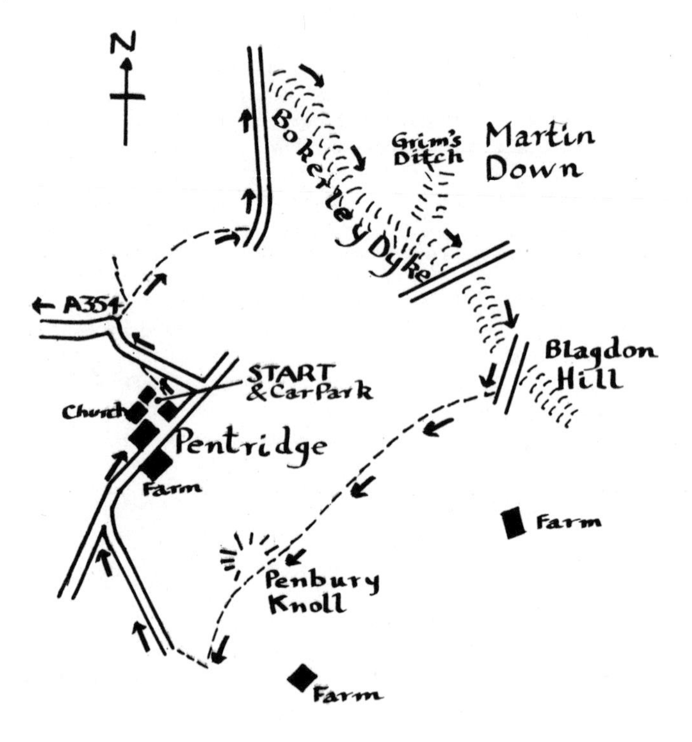
N
Bokerley Dyke
Grim's Ditch
Martin Down
A354
START & Car Park
Church
Pentridge
Farm
Blagdon Hill
Farm
Penbury Knoll
Farm

WALK ONE

Cranborne Chase

Introduction: Ancient earthworks are so common on Cranborne Chase in the north east corner of Dorset that the area is virtually an open air museum of archaeology!

Even the walker whose anticipation of antiquities has so often been rewarded by a 'heap of stones' or a 'bump in the field' should not be disappointed by Cranborne Chase. In a remarkably small area there is a Bronze Age cursus or processional way, an Iron Age hill fort, the finest stretch of Roman road in the country and Bokerley Dyke, an impressive Romano-British boundary that runs across the country for five miles. And there are umpteen barrows.

The Chase is ideal walking country, with long views in all directions and a network of footpaths, criss-crossing firm downland turf. Bokerley Dyke forms the border between Dorset and Hampshire.

On the Hampshire side is Martin Down, a National Nature Reserve.

Distance: A relatively easy circular walk covering about 4½ miles (7km) of tracks and downland. It should take about 2½ hours. O.S. map, 1:50,000, Sheet 184.

Refreshments: Unfortunately there are no cafes or pubs along the route.

How to get there: Turn left to Pentridge from the A354 Salisbury-Blandford road, which passes from Wiltshire into the so-called 'Martin peninsula' of Hampshire and then into Dorset. The Pentridge turning is found after passing through Woodyates. Follow the road down to a T-junction and turn right into the village. After a short distance there is a turning right signposted to the church and village hall. There is limited parking space by the village green.

The walk: The walk starts in the field to the right (north east) of the village hall. With the church behind, walk into the field and then turn left and keep to the hedge until reaching a stile at the top, beside the road leading from the A354. Turn left on the road and then on a sharp left-hand bend take a bridleway that turns off to the right and runs between tall hedges. The route keeps to it for about half a mile, ignoring a fork to the left after about 100 yards.

To the right in the distance are the grassy slopes of Bokerley Down, whilst to the left are the farm lands of Woodyates. The hedges are rich with a variety of different shrubs, suggesting that they are very old. Buckthorn, elder, hawthorn and ilex crowd the sides of the path, intertwined with bramble and bryony and great banks of old man's beard.

The bridleway meets a track at a T-junction. Here the route turns left onto the track, which it follows round for a short distance to the Dorset-Hampshire border and Bokerley Dyke. This great defence work is preceded by a slighter bank on the right and burial tumuli on the left – the first of many to be seen!

The view is superb across Martin Down, a National Nature Reserve, towards Salisbury, with the prominent mass of Windmill Hill in the middle distance.

A footpath runs along the Hampshire side of the dyke and comes to a group of tumuli on the left. They stand beside a slighter earthwork which runs at right angles to the dyke and is called (like so many) Grim's Ditch. This is a fragment of a defence work that seems to have stretched across to the River Avon north of Downton. The route continues beside the dyke (or on the top) and crosses a track leading from a patch of woodland to the right. As it approaches a second patch of woodland, a prominent '2nd line of defence' can be seen to the right. At the far side of the wood it meets a track that cuts through the rampart at the foot of Blagdon (meaning Black Down) Hill. Here the route turns right and after a short distance right again through a field gate (ignoring an acute right-hand turn onto another path).

The path continues along the right-hand side of the field, with Blagdon Farm down to the left. It crosses a steeplechaser's stile and shortly after passing an old chalk pit on the left crosses a similar stile in the fence to the right. The path hugs the other side of this fence as it climbs to the woody summit of Penbury Knoll along the escarpment of Pentridge Hill. To the right are the clear marks of old field boundaries that stretch up to the ramparts of an old camp on the hill. Archaeologists say that the camp dates from the Iron Age and one of the banks is a remnant of the 'park pale' belonging to a medieval deer park on Blagdon Hill. This covered a thousand acres and was one of the greatest deer parks in Dorset.

The view from Penbury Knoll is perhaps the best in our 'open air museum of archaeology'. In one direction there is a grandstand view of Bokerley Dyke, whilst to the west can be seen the distinct line of Ackling Dyke, a substantial remnant of the Roman road that ran in a dog-leg between Old Sarum (the pre-medieval site of Salisbury) and Dorchester, via Badbury Rings. On the horizon is Wor Barrow, a Neolithic burial mound that stands close to a group of younger, Bronze Age barrows on Oakley Down.

The route continues along the southern edge of the knoll, over one steeplechaser's stile at the edge of the trees and across the turf of Pentridge Hill to another similar stile. Here the path turns through a right-angle and keeps to the field boundary until it soon meets a track. This continues to the foot of the hill, where it meets another track from the left and continues through the yard of Pentridge Farm. After a short distance the farm road meets the track on the left that leads back to the village green.

Historical Notes

Pentridge: The village has two connections with literary figures, one of which is spurious. William Barnes the dialect Dorset poet wrote of 'Pentridge Farm', but this fictional place was based on a farm elsewhere in Dorset, in the Vale of Blackmoor, at his own birthplace near Sturminster Newton.

The other connection, with the poet Robert Browning, is real. Although both his father and grandfather worked in London at the Bank of England, his family came from Woodyates, near Pentridge. A tablet beside the chancel arch of the church says that the 'first known forefather' of the poet was a namesake who died here in November 1746. He was his great-great-grandfather, whose son Thomas kept the Woodyates Inn, which once stood alongside the Salisbury-Dorchester road. This hostelry was well-known for its association with the ill-fated Duke of Monmouth, whose Protestant rebellion of 1685 failed. This pretender to the throne came to the Woodyates Inn to escape after the fiasco of the Battle of Sedgemoor. Here he rested and dressed as a shepherd, before being eventually captured near Horton Heath on the county borders.

Martin Down is now in Hampshire, but in the lifetime of Caleb Bawcombe, who is depicted in W.H. Hudson's *A Shepherd's Life*, it was in Wiltshire. He clearly loved this countryside and once remarked: 'We must take what is sent. But if 'twas offered to me and I was told to choose my work, I'd say, "Give me my Wiltsheer Downs again and let me be a shepherd there all my life long".'

In fact, the unique turf of the down, created over centuries by grazing, would by now have been modified beyond repair if the Nature Conservancy Council and Hampshire County Council had not in 1978 acquired it and returned it to sheep. The flexi-fencing that now plays the part of Caleb's hurdles is systematically moved over much of the 625-acre site to allow sheep to chew off large plants and thereby protect the rich assembly of chalkland herbs. There are nine species of orchid to be found here (but not picked) and several rare species of butterfly, including the silver-spotted skipper and the Adonis blue. Birds include the nightingale, lesser whitethroat and hen harrier, with occasional visits by the stone curlew. You may be lucky and see a roe deer.

Bokerley Dyke: This massive rampart was once the frontier between the Romano-British people of Dorset and the Saxons of Wessex. The traditional view of the conquering of England by the Saxons, based on the Anglo-Saxon Chronicle, is that they landed on the Hampshire coast in AD 495 and fought their way inland. The archaeological record, however, suggests that Saxons were present in Hampshire before this date and probably first came as mercenaries to defend the local populace against piracy after the withdrawal of the Roman forces at the end of the fourth century.

It was at about this time (c. AD 370) that Bokerley Dyke was first constructed by the Roman authorities to prevent incursions from the southwest. The great bank blocked the Roman road between *Durnovaria* (Dorchester) and *Sarum* (Old Sarum) and provided a line of defence five miles long between Blagdon Hill and the high lands of the more northerly parts of Cranborne Chase. It was a sort of 'Hadrian's Wall' of the southwest.

The Roman road was later re-opened but was then closed again, an act that effectively cut off communications to the south-west and brought about the decay of the road. Today, only small sections remain.

The most important point about the Bokerley Dyke frontier was that it allowed the peoples of what became Dorset to continue their

Romanised way of life, independent of the Saxon warlords, for more than two centuries after most of the rest of Southern England had been conquered. The West Saxons first occupied Hampshire and Wiltshire before turning to Gloucestershire and Somerset. But the men of Dorset who defended Bokerley Dyke resisted until perhaps the late sixth century. They then retreated about 15 miles to a defensive position called Combs Ditch. This runs for about three miles along a ridge above the valley of the Stour, north east of Winterborne Whitechurch.

Cranborne Chase: Although antiquaries such as William Stukeley had long noted the rich assemblies of ancient earthworks in the Cranborne Chase area, it was not until about a century ago that any scientifically respectable work was done. By good fortune, Lt-Gen Augustus Fox-Lane a soldier turned archaeologist then inherited the Rivers estate, which included much of Cranborne Chase. The general adopted the name Pitt-Rivers and systematically carried out a number of classic excavations here in the 1880s.

These digs established Pitt-Rivers as the 'father of British archaeology.' He was the first Inspector of Ancient Monuments to be appointed, in 1882, and his collections of ethnographic material from all round the world became the basis for the Pitt-Rivers Museum, Oxford.

One who was greatly influenced by Pitt-Rivers and carried on his work was George Heywood Sumner, who lived in the New Forest and in 1913 published *The Ancient Earthworks of Cranborne Chase.* This was one of the first systematic surveys of earthworks to be carried out in Britain and was a remarkable feat for one man.

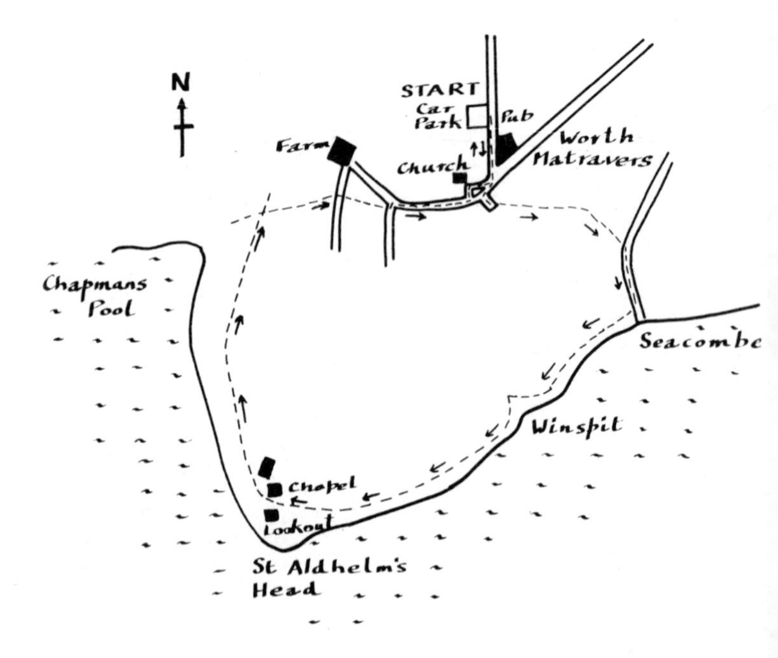
N
START
Car Park
Pub
Farm
Church
Worth Matravers
Chapmans Pool
Seacombe
Winspit
Chapel
Lookout
St Aldhelm's Head

WALK TWO

St Aldhelm's Head and The Purbeck Coast

Introduction: The coast of Dorset is generally reckoned to be one of the most beautiful in the country. This walk is a small part of the Dorset Coast Path, a popular long-distance route that starts at Shell Bay, at the western entrance to Poole Harbour, and runs without a break to the county border at Lyme Regis.

Dorset's coastal scenery has resulted from the drowning of rolling downland due to rises in sea level. The steep slopes of the downs and the sheer white cliffs at their edge provide all the elements of a dramatic landscape that is ideal for walking.

Distance: About 4 miles (6½ km) in a circular route. It takes about 2 hours. O.S. map, 1:50,000, Sheet 195.

Refreshments: Square and Compass Inn, Worth Matravers.

How to get there: From Poole take the A35 towards Bere Regis and Dorchester and then turn onto the A351 near Lychett Minster and continue to Wareham. Follow the signs to Corfe Castle on the A351 and just beyond Corfe turn right onto the B3069. This leads to a steep S-bend into Kingston. Keep left in the village centre and after a mile turn right to Worth Matravers. There is a small car park on the right, just after entering the village.

The walk: Turn right out of the car park and walk into the centre of the village. The road passes the Square and Compass Inn, which takes its name from the tools of the quarryman, whose trade until the 1940s dominated the life of Worth Matravers. The attractive stone houses of the village and the dry-stone walls hereabouts were no doubt built from quarry scrap (and perhaps look all the better for that).

Crab and lobster have also provided a livelihood here, as in many seaside villages in the West Country. The willows that still grow in the centre of the village (behind the bus shelter) were planted to provide the withies used in making lobster pots.

The first part of the walk to Seacombe starts in a short cul-de-sac that turns left opposite the bus shelter. It is a well-marked route and after a few yards ascends a few steps and runs as a narrow way between gardens. It emerges on the edge of a steep dry valley, which is marked with a series of worn terraces. These are called lynchets and are relics of medieval farming. Continuous ploughing of long strips of land pushed the earth to one side, forming the steep banks that can still be seen here and at several other places along the walk.

There is a clear path across the valley between the lynchets, suggesting that the way to Seacombe is an ancient route. It continues over a stile in a dry-stone wall, across a field and into a small valley via another stile. It then leads downhill, crosses the bed of a small stream and turns right along a narrow combe to the sea (hence the name Seacombe!). The route is marked on the small 'milestones' that are found along the Dorset Coast Walk. 'Winspit ¾ mile,' says one just before reaching the sea, where our path turns off to the right up a steep flight of steps to the clifftop.

But before taking this direction it is worth continuing to the sea and looking out on the grand limestone cliffs of Seacombe. They and other local quarries were once worked for Portland Stone, which was used for building and making such things as granary staddlestones and stone sinks. The great caverns blasted out by the quarriers can still be seen, but they should NOT be entered. Stone stacks were left for support, but they are not safe. Amongst the wildlife which now makes use of some of these old workings is the rare Greater Horseshoe Bat.

The path to Winspit brings rich rewards for the walker's habit of 'looking back': easily missed are the huge caves which undercut the cliff at Seacombe.

Winspit gives the impression of having been a largish quarrying centre; it is also a very pretty spot. A great part of the cliff by the sea has been cut away and contains what looks like a ruined quarrier's cottage, but is probably a military relic. During the last war this part of the coast and the land behind was occupied by an RAF Telecommunications Research Establishment, which played an important part in the development of radar. There are further signs of the old camp beyond Winspit, near a coastguard station on the high cliff of St Aldhelm's Head. But the highlight of this well known viewpoint is the little square chapel which stands there.

The path continues along the cliffs to a beautiful little cove called Chapman's Pool. It is a route that walkers will find challenging, particularly at an apparently nameless valley that ought perhaps to be called Tough Climb Combe! The path turns right 'halfway' along the rim of the little cove and continues across farmlands towards a prominent silage tower, leaving the buildings of Renscombe Farm on the left. A minor road runs beside the tower and back to Worth Matravers. In the village the road forks left to the church and then continues to the village centre and hence back to the car park via the Square and Compass Inn.

Historical Notes

The quarriers: Purbeck 'marble' and Portland stone were for centuries the second most important source of income in Dorset, bettered only by farming. Purbeck marble was the first of the two to be widely used, for monuments and small architectural items such as pillars. The rough-hewn stone was taken off by sea or carted to Corfe for dressing and finishing by the 'marblers' who lived there in the shadow of the famous castle. Westminster Abbey and many cathedrals around the country contain Purbeck marble, including Canterbury, Winchester, Salisbury, Wells, Exeter and Worcester.

The Jurassic limestone quarries at Seacombe, Winspit and elsewhere provided a type of Portland Stone which was much-used from the seventeenth century for public buildings. The architect Inigo Jones chose Portland Stone for the Westminster Banqueting Hall and it was also used by Sir Christopher Wren for St Paul's and many other City churches.

Worth Matravers has its roots as a Saxon settlement that took the name *worth*, meaning an enclosure or farmstead. The second element in its name comes from a short period in the fourteenth century when John Matravers was lord of the manor.

Until about 1500 Worth Matravers was more important than neighbouring Swanage, which only justified a chapel to the mother church. A local footpath that ran between the two communities is still called Priest's Way.

St Nicholas's Church is a good example of how country churches were sometimes 'patched up' with 'throw outs' from elsewhere. The impressively triply dog-toothed chancel arch has been so designated by experts, who point out that on the west side are recesses for side altars that could not have been present in the small church. The finely carved south door (said to have been defaced by Cromwellian soldiers) is also thought to have come from elsewhere. However, there are some Early Norman windows and other elements in the church fabric which testify to its age.

On the north side of Worth Matravers church is the grave of Benjamin Jesty, the man who was, as an inscription says, 'the first person (known) that introduced the Cow Pox by inoculation . . .' He lived at Downshay Manor, a mile and a half to the north east of the village, and earned his living as a farmer. Before this he lived at Yetminster, in the north of the county, and it was here that he carried out his bold experiment more than 20 years before the celebrated work of Edward Jenner, generally regarded as the discoverer of vaccination. Admittedly Jesty's 'medicine' was a bit crude: he took a 'stocking needle' infected with matter from a cow with the pox and scratched the arms of his 'willing' wife and two of their children. The idea behind the experiment was based on the well-known observation that milk maids never caught smallpox.

In the week following the inoculation Benjamin's wife became extremely ill and he was obliged to call in a doctor. He is said to have remarked: 'You have done a bold thing, Mr Jesty, but I will get you through if I can,' a comment which betrays a certain lack of concern for the poor woman herself, who many years later was buried beside her husband at Worth Matravers.

St Aldhelm's Head takes its name from the remarkable first Bishop of Sherborne, who was appointed in 705 AD to a diocese that probably then included the whole of Dorset, Somerset, Devon and Cornwall.

The small square chapel that now stands on the headland is thought to date from the late twelfth century and may have been served by an anchoress who performed masses in the manner of chantries elsewhere. Support for this theory came in 1957 when part of a gravestone in Purbeck marble was found by a farmer and later excavations unearthed the bones of a woman. The remnants of what might have been her 'cell' were also discovered. The gravestone can now be seen in Worth Maltravers church.

WALK THREE

The North Dorset Downs

Introduction: The North Dorset Downs are the backbone of the county. They start a few miles to the west of Blandford Forum and stretch to the western borders – an extensive area of uplifted chalk lands which provide the rambler with some of the finest walking country in Britain. There are miles and miles of remote paths with breathtaking views over the Dorset lowlands, for most of the people here live in villages on the edges of the chalk or in the river valleys. The land is drained to the south by the rivers Piddle and Frome, which meet at Wareham and discharge into Poole Harbour, which is a drowned estuary.

The downs are characterised by extremely steep slopes, at the foot of which run small sunken lanes that add to the overall sense of remoteness. The excitement of walking in this part of the county often comes from the great contrast between the wide open views seen from the hills and the shut-in shut-out, almost claustrophobic feel of some of the smaller hamlets. This is a walk for those who enjoy being 'away from it all'.

Distance: About 5½ miles (9 km) in a circular route. It will take about 2½ hours. O.S. map, 1:50,000, Sheet 194.

Refreshments: In Ibberton, close to the church, is The Crown pub, whilst nearby on Ibberton Hill, with 'the best view in Dorset', is a restaurant, Baker's Folly, which particularly boasts 'Sunday lunches and cream teas.'

How to get there: The walk starts at a Dorsetshire County Council car park at Okeford Hill, a mile to the north of Turnworth. From Blandford Forum, take the Dorchester road across the river Stour and turn right to Winterborne Stickland. Turn right again at a

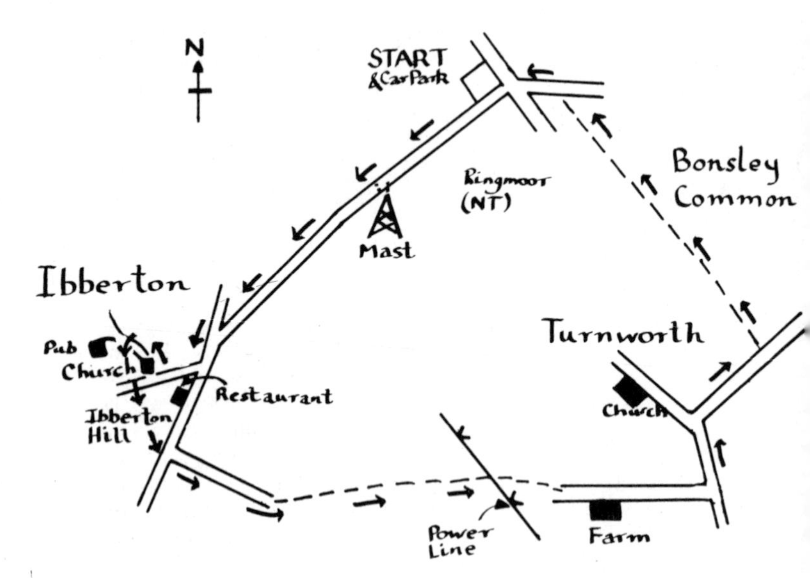

T-junction just before the village and follow the road for 3 miles, through Turnworth. The car park is on the left, at the top of a steep hill.

The walk: To the south of the car park a bridle-path leads to the west, towards a signposted picnic area. Like so many old routes, it runs along a ridgeway with superb views on both sides, particularly to the right. The steep escarpment of the chalk provides one of the finest views in Dorset, across to the Vale of Blackmoor to the north and west.

After about half a mile there is a turning to the left, through a gate and past a dew-pond, to Ringmoor, a large area of land owned by the National Trust. Walkers with a particular interest in archaeology may find it worthwhile to take a detour to the left to survey the humps and bumps of a prehistoric settlement site, though the main walk continues along the ridge for another mile.

After passing a prominent mast, the path loses some of the superb panorama that has been with it since Okeford Hill and descends to a minor road above the village of Ibberton. The path turns left onto the road and then after a few hundred yards turns right onto a tiny road which falls with an alarming gradient down Ibberton Hill. (A short distance further on along the minor road is the Baker's Folly Restaurant, which serves good food in a dining room that has superb views of the North Dorset lowlands, stretching through Hazelbury Bryan to the Vale of Blackmoor. Note also the Crown pub below.) Half-way down Ibberton Hill there is a short-cut to the village via a halter path that turns off to the right, opposite a small cliff on the left.

The path drops past the church, which is reached through a small iron turnstile. Just past the church, on the right, is a small Wesleyan chapel, built in 1884, and now converted to a private house. Beyond that is the village itself, with its pub, the Crown.

The route continues by doubling back along the halter path to the small cliff referred to above. Here the path continues on the opposite side of the road, where there are two farm gates at right angles. The right of way turns sharp left, over both gates, and continues along a marked hollow way, with a field boundary to the right. It passes under power lines and emerges into an open field. Here it continues half-left, back to the top of Ibberton Hill, where there is a prominent bridleway sign.

The bridleway continues opposite, via a gravelled track which runs east from the middle of a small picnic area. It continues from the top of Ibberton Hill in a more or less straight line for more than a mile to the east. A marked track gives way to a gate and an unmarked route across grassland and through a crop field. Keeping two patches of woodland to the left, the walker should make for a farm which lies in a hollow ahead. The route skirts a small, steep dry valley coming in from the right at a point where the path runs under power lines. It is a land of wide open views.

The path continues along a marked track to the farm and then continues along its access track to meet the road south of Turnworth. Here it turns left onto the road and after a quarter of a mile turns right along a signposted bridleway.

The road continues to Turnworth about a quarter of a mile ahead, whose church is of some interest for its connections with Thomas Hardy, and may be worth a detour.

Returning to the main route, this goes uphill along the bridleway, past farm buildings and then after a further 200 yards turns left on a bridleway that runs between fields. Soon it meets the woodlands of Bonsley Common and keeps to the left-hand edge of the trees for half a mile. If time allows, there is a network of paths which enable the woods to be explored.

Beyond the woodland the walk runs alongside a thick hedge on the right until it reaches woodland once more, where it crosses to the other side of the hedge. It continues along a forestry track until it meets another track in a T-junction. Turning left brings the walk full circuit, back to the car park at Okeford Hill.

Historical Notes

Ringmoor: This is a rare example of an Iron Age or Romano-British settlement, according to the National Trust, who own the site. Although the humps and bumps that remain are not obvious, they reveal apparently that there were two small circular enclosures with about 30 acres of associated Celtic fields. Perhaps the people who once occupied Ringmoor would have lived like their contemporaries at Pimperne, just outside Blandford Forum, whose way of life has been re-created in Hampshire, at the Butser Iron Age Farm, near Petersfield.

Ibberton is a delightful village that clusters at the foot of the northern escarpment of the downs. Climbing Ibberton Hill in a modern car is a hairy experience and it must have been unbelievably difficult with horses, particularly in winter. Perhaps it was rarely necessary, for the village 'looks out' to Hazelbury Bryan (Thomas Hardy's 'Nuzzlebury') and the Blackmoor Vale.

St Eustace Church, Ibberton, overlooks the main village in a position that seems to emphasise its spiritual authority. The path to it is so steep that when the church virtually collapsed in 1889, villagers must have quite welcomed the 'tin tabernacle' (now the village hall) that took its place for a while. Perhaps their feelings were mixed when the old church was re-opened after extensive renovation in 1909. (Interestingly, in the interim marriages continued to be solemnised in the ruins.)

A hint of how the locals lived is given by the huge two-handled cider pitcher that now stands in the north aisle. At Christmas this was taken to local farms to be filled for the bell-ringers, whose 'changes' were no doubt much enlivened! A notable feature of the church is its clock, a memorial to the large number of men from

Ibberton and the neighbouring hamlet of Belchalwall who fell in the First World War. The 'thud! thud!' of the clock's mechanism is extremely loud inside the small church and its chime is deafening!

The church is rare in Britain for its dedication to St Eustace, the Roman general whose conversion to Christianity led to a fearful death. A spring below the church also takes its name, 'Stachy's Well', from the church's dedication and hints that mysticism and perhaps local pilgrimage were part of Ibberton's past.

Turnworth is typical of many villages in Dorset, whose growth was constrained to a line by the steepness of the hills on either side. The village fields were on this higher land and Turnworth Down is quoted as an example of Celtic fields (probably related to the Ringmoor settlement mentioned above) overlain with the ridge-and-furrow of later medieval farmers. These later fields, however, were only used for a short period and show how villages would take land into cultivation as required.

St Mary's Church, Turnworth, is one of the few buildings to show the architectural work of Thomas Hardy. He designed the leafy Gothic capitals of the church during 1868-69, just after the death of John Hicks, whose firm in Dorchester employed the novelist-to-be.

Turnworth House nearby was worked into *The Woodlanders*, published in 1887, where it is depicted as Great Hintock House.

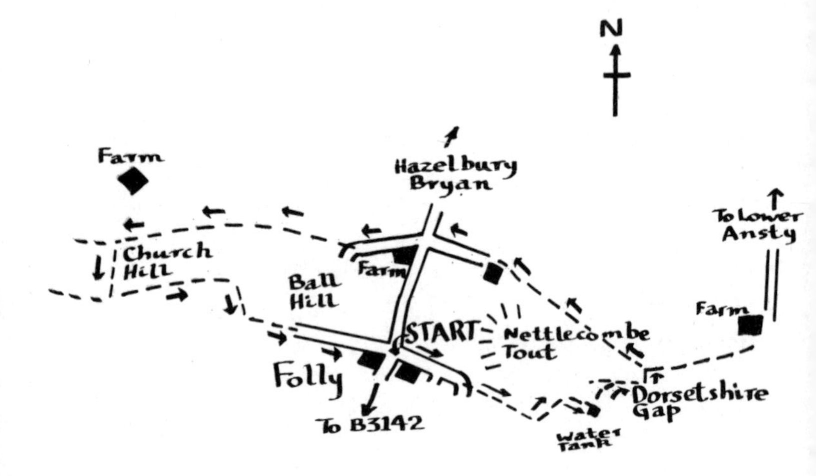

N
Farm
Hazelbury Bryan
To Lower Ansty
Church Hill
Farm
Ball Hill
START
Nettlecombe Tout
Farm
Folly
Dorsetshire Gap
To B3142
Water Tank

Folly and The Dorsetshire Gap

Introduction: The north eastern corner of the North Dorset Downs is marked by the 'unremitting' steepness of Ibberton, Woolland and Bulbarrow, the last of which is the highest hill in Dorset. The first break in this impressive escarpment is made by the valley of a small stream called the Devil's Brook. From its source near Ansty it flows into the Piddle between Tolpuddle and Puddletown. En route it skirts those skittishly named villages, Melcombe Bingham and Bingham's Melcombe.

The next block of downland to the west stretches to Cerne Abbas and the valley of the river Cerne. It also includes some impressive north-facing scarp slopes, albeit retreated a mile or so to the south. Also contained within this area is a quirk of geology where steep slopes meet within a small area, as if some giant had folded the chalk like a pocket handkerchief. This is called the Dorsetshire Gap and no walker in the county can really consider himself to have earned his boots until he has been there.

The Gap can be reached from Ansty and Melcombe Bingham, but this walk covers a particularly remote area that lies between Melcombe and Buckland Newton.

Distance: About 4 miles (6½km) of fairly energetic walking along a circular route. It can probably be done in 2 hours, but the views could delay the dreamy walker for another hour or more. O.S. map, 1:50,000, Sheet 194.

Refreshments: There are none on the walk as described, but a footpath leads from the Dorsetshire Gap via Cothayes Farm to Lower Ansty, where there is an excellent freehouse, The Fox Inn.

How to get there: From Blandford Forum, take the A357 to

Sturminster Newton, continuing past the turning right into the town. After about half a mile, turn left to Hazelbury Bryan. Bear right to Mappowder and continue for 2 miles to the hamlet of Folly, under the steep shoulder of Nettlecombe Tout to the left. There is limited parking on the verge.

The walk: Take a track to the left at Folly (running east) and keep climbing, ignoring a track turning to the right after about a quarter of a mile. After a similar distance the track itself turns to the right, but the path continues uphill, along the right-hand side of a strip of woodland. Walking in the field alongside is much easier than following the path, which has become somewhat overgrown.

From this height there are superb views towards Ball Hill to the west and north to the plains of the Vale of Blackmoor. The spur of chalk immediately to the north is called Nettlecombe Tout and must have been, as its name suggests, a fine lookout. An ancient ditch completes the defence of this Iron Age site.

At the top left-hand corner of the field is a gate, followed shortly by another gate. After passing through these, the path turns left around the perimeter of a field and then turns right towards a prominent water tank. At the tank it turns left across a crop field to another gate, downhill through another crop field along a marked sunken track and through yet another gate into a patch of woodland. Hereafter, the walk keeps to the sunken track for some distance, until met by a similar track coming in from the left. At this point, turn left to the Dorsetshire Gap.

The best way to appreciate this curious geological formation is to mount one of the slopes. This unfolds a breathtaking view to the north and east, though the steep shoulder of Bulbarrow to the right looks deceptively tame. Below is the wooded spread of Melcombe Park.

It is, it must be admitted, a little disappointing to find no public sign or other mark of recognition at this 'most Dorset' of spots. There was at one time a visitors' book at the Gap so that walkers could at least prove that they had been there. The curious downfolds in the chalk look almost as if they had been contrived for some mystical purpose! Humps and bumps in the chalk suggest that ancient man may, too, have been impressed by this curious spot.

The sunken track that leads to the Gap is terminated by a gate, to the left of which runs a footpath. It disappears into woodland and continues under a steep bank to a field. Keeping woodland to the left, the route continues to a gate, where a new view unfolds of the lands to the west, across the Blackmoor Vale towards Sherborne and the northern borders of the county. At the western end of the wood (behind which lies Nettlecombe Tout) the path continues around the right-hand side of a farm building and along its access track, towards the steep slopes of Ball Hill.

Ahead is Armswell Farm, which stands alongside the road to Folly (reached by turning left). The next part of the walk passes along the right-hand sides of the wooded slopes of Ball Hill and Church Hill. The track that leads through the farm yard turns to the left after a short distance, whereas our path keeps straight on. At the far end of Ball Hill it continues across a cow down and rises to a new view to the west.

Halfway along the northern edge of Church Hill, beyond a farm which lies in a hollow, a small gate leads into the woodland to the left. It stands just beyond a field gate, where the boundary of the woodland juts out over a small area. The small gate leads to a steep path, which goes through the wood and emerges in a crop field.

The final leg of the walk follows the southern edge of Church Hill and descends to Folly. The path turns left at the crop field and passes between the woodland of the hill and another patch of woodland which comes in on the right-hand side. A track then leads along the edge of the second piece of woodland, leaving it at a gate to start the downward path across grassland to Folly.

To the right lie the slopes of Higher Hill, criss-crossed by the clear lines of ancient tracks. These high lands have no doubt literally served as highways since the very earliest times.

The final leg continues downhill along a 'scramble' path and sunken lane to the tiny hamlet of Folly.

Historical Notes

Nettlecombe Tout contains the traces of an uncompleted hill fort with a single ditch that encloses an area of about 15 acres. The work was never completed. There are other earthworks to the south east of Folly that may have been related to the fort. Excavations at Bowden's Hill a mile to the south of Nettlecombe Tout have revealed evidence of occupation in the Late Bronze Age or Iron Age, around 600 BC.

Sites such as Nettlecombe Tout have suggested to archaeologists that man once dwelt mainly on the tops of hills, but more recently it has been argued that the valleys were equally important, but that later cultivation has destroyed almost all the evidence in these parts.

Melcombe Horsey is the name of the parish which includes the western part of this walk. It takes its name from the manor house at Higher Melcombe, built in the middle of the sixteenth century for Sir John Horsey, a friend of Sir Walter Raleigh, whose most celebrated house is at Clifton Maybank, west of Sherborne. The parish also includes Melcombe Bingham, which contains the house called Bingham's Melcombe, where one of Dorset's great families, the Binghams, lived for 600 years. The present house dates from about 1500, and is not open to view.

The tiny church of St Andrew in the grounds can, however, be visited. It contains memorials to the Binghams, including one to a child who lived for only 7 months in the early years of the eighteenth century, his mother requesting that his dust remain undisturbed. There is a memorial to one of the family, Sir Richard Bingham, in Westminster Abbey. In 1571 he fought against the Turks at Lepanto in the same battle in which Cervantes, the author of *Don Quixote*, lost the use of his left hand.

Clouds Hill and T.E. Lawrence

Introduction: Visitors to St Martin's church, Wareham, may be struck by the fine effigy of T.E. Lawrence, carved by the sculptor Eric Kennington. The reasons why the man who found fame amongst the sands of Arabia sought the sands of Dorset can be found by travelling a few miles to the west, to the lands dominated by the presence of the Royal Armoured Corps at Bovington Camp.

The RAC Tank Museum to the south of the camp is one of Dorset's most successful tourist attractions, but to the north is a fine area for walkers, almost as remote as T.E. Lawrence found it in 1923 when he sought refuge from the camp where he was serving.

The heathlands of the Poole Basin (Thomas Hardy's 'Egdon Heath') are the largest single area of this sort of habitat outside the New Forest.

Distance: A circular route of about 5 miles (8 km) over easy ground. Walking time, about 2 hours, O.S. map, 1:50,000. Sheet 194.

Refreshments: Unfortunately there are no pubs or cafes along the route, but Bovington can provide the walker with the essentials of life.

How to get there: The walk starts from a small car park, about 500 yards to the north of Bovington Camp on the east side of the road. This can be reached either from the A35 Poole-Dorchester road, via Briantspuddle and Throop Heath, or from the A352 Wareham-Wool road, following signs to Bovington. There is public transport to the camp itself from neighbouring towns.

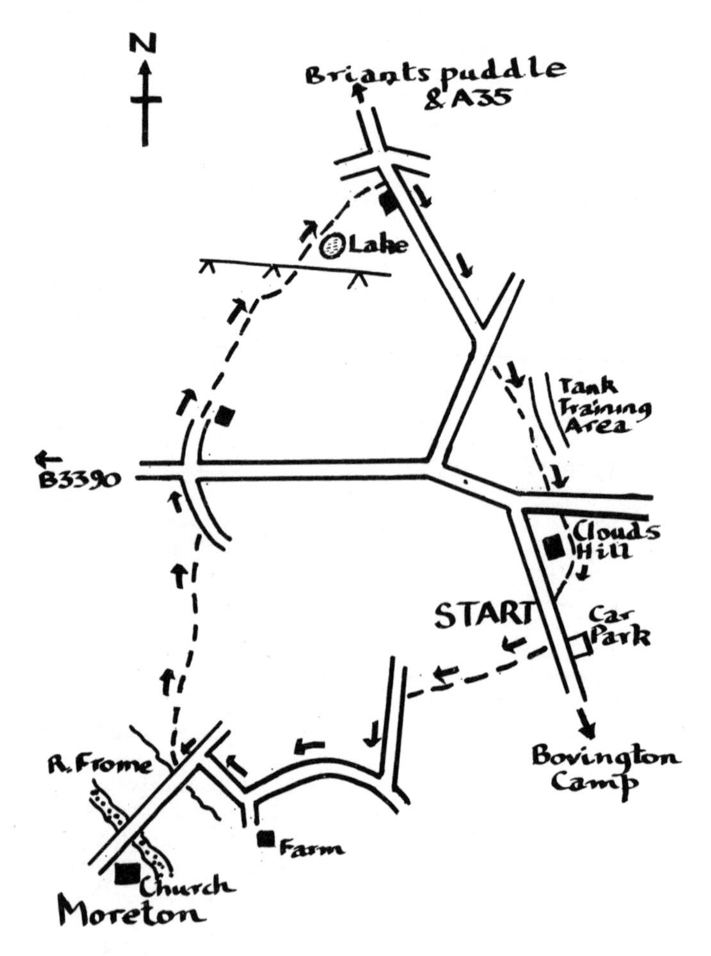

The walk: The starting point overlooks a military wasteland, where the manoeuvres of tanks have churned up the native Dorset heath to a fine mess. Cross the road (or stay and watch the tanks for a while!) and take a waymarked path which runs to the west.

Traces of the Army are soon left behind, for the path enters woodland to the right, just where a block of woodland on the left comes to an end. To the south are views of the downs that protect this part of Dorset from the sea.

The footpath curves round out into the open once more before becoming a fully-fledged woodland path, which runs into the trees on the right. It falls for about a quarter of a mile, through rhododendron undercover which is a mass of blossom in the early summer. At the point where it meets a track at a T-junction, turn left and walk between woods of conifer and silver birch. Another track is soon met: turn right and continue through woodland and out into open farmland.

The path meets a gravelled track, with Snelling farm to the left. The walker should now turn right, along the access track of the farm, towards distant power lines, and then left at a T-junction. Ahead is a carrier of the river Frome and the river itself, as it skirts the village of Moreton, where T.E. Lawrence is buried. The walk, however, turns to the right just before the carrier, near the remains of a sluice, which was once used to flood the nearby meadows. There are two footpaths which run from this point: our path strikes out to the right and clips the edge of a patch of woodland. It crosses a stile into a cornfield and then makes through the crop towards woodland. This is one of the few fields where the corn is still gathered into sheaves by hand, probably to preserve the stalks for thatching.

The walk continues over two small drainage channels and into the woodland, a mixture of oak, silver birch and conifers, with rhododendron undercover. It is the start of an extensive tract of Forestry Commission land. A peaty path winds amongst the trees, but the chances of getting lost are reduced by helpful yellow arrows! The path emerges onto a track: turn left and continue for about a quarter of a mile to the road. Cross over and take a bridleway signposted to the Cullpeppers Dish, through Oakers Wood.

The track soon narrows to a path through a tunnel of trees laced with rhododendron bushes and then comes to a gate. Here the route turns half-right towards a power line, with a marked firebreak to the right. The walk keeps between conifer plantations and rises towards a bank overlooking Rimsmoor Pond, a marshy area of water flecked with tufts of Bog Cotton.

The walk, marked with yellow arrows, slips off to the right a short distance beyond the pond and continues alongside houses to a minor road, meeting it just to the south of a crossroads. For about half a mile the walk keeps to this road, until it meets another road at a fork. Cross over to the other side of the junction and take a footpath into scrubland. This is a typical Dorset heathland, a blend of bracken, conifers, heather and sand. To the north can be seen the higher lands towards Black Hill and the valley of the Piddle.

The path soon comes to the edge of part of the circuit used by the tanks from Bovington, but after about 200 yards a grassy track slips off to the right and continues up a steep bank through trees to a minor road. If you have navigated correctly you should come out close to a T-junction, to the south-east of which lies Clouds Hill, the cottage once owned by T.E. Lawrence and now kept by the National Trust. In fact, the most likely track you are likely to take across this bare heathland comes out slightly to the east of the junction. A footpath continues up a bank on the other side of the road and makes its way behind Clouds Hill, through ferny scrubland and back to the car park where the walk started.

Historical Notes

Clouds Hill and Bovington Camp: The camp has been the home of the Royal Armoured Corps since the 1920s. Many people come to see the Tank Museum, which boasts the largest collection of armoured fighting vehicles in the world.

T.E. Lawrence was serving as a private in the Tank Corps at Bovington in the very early days of the camp when he rented the cottage Clouds Hill. He needed a place to get away from camp life and to enable him to work on his *Seven Pillars of Widsom*. He wrote: 'I don't sleep here, but come out at 4.30 pm till 9 pm nearly every night, and dream, or write or read by the fire, or play Beethoven and Mozart to myself on the box.' His music room, smelling of smoke, is still there, upstairs, with its huge gramophone horn and an ancient Royal typewriter. It is open to the rafters and has such unusual features as wooden shutters rather than curtains and a door consisting of leather stretched across an iron frame.

Lawrence was obviously fascinated by new materials and quirky DIY touches, for one small room with a bunk is lined with aluminium asbestos foil and lighted by a porthole! The house does not, however, have a kitchen. Food, it seems, was prepared as a picnic on the fire, and 'stuffed olives, salted almonds and Heinz baked beans' were regularly on the menu.

Clouds Hill is an extremely modest cottage by any standard: a cream-washed, tile-roofed dwelling with the Book Room and a bathroom downstairs and the Music Room and Bunk Room upstairs. A hint that it is something special comes from the inscription in Greek over the front door, which translates as: 'Why worry?' or 'Nothing matters'.

The Book Room is a booklover's paradise and is almost filled by a huge leather-covered divan. It is furnished with the sort of things that boys tend to bring home from CTD (craft, technology and design) classes, including a fender and candlestick in wrought iron and an oak chest. There are illustrations from Lawrence's thesis on crusader castles, published in 1913, photographs from the Schneider Race of 1929, in which he was involved, and paintings by Augustus John and others.

Lawrence took his discharge from the Services in February 1935 and came to Clouds Hill. In May he was severely injured in an accident on the high-powered motor-cycle he loved. He was returning along the road that leads across the heath from the camp and swerved to avoid two young cyclists. A few days later he died in the hospital at Bovington, and was buried nearby at Moreton.

T.E. Lawrence's funeral at Moreton church was attended by the King of Iraq, though his grave was originally only marked by a simple wooden cross. This was later replaced by a stone which was set up and designed by his friend Eric Kennington. The inscription refers to Lawrence simply as a 'Fellow of All Souls College, Oxford' and a footstone depicts an open book with the motto of Oxford University Press, *Dominus Illuminatio Mea*.

Clouds Hill is owned by the National Trust and is open to view on Wednesdays, Thursdays, Fridays, Sundays and Bank Holiday Mondays, 2-5 pm, during April-September, and on Sundays only, 1-4 pm, for the rest of the year.

Moreton is skirted on this walk and is well worth a short detour to visit it. The lord of the manor seems for centuries to have been called James Frampton: there was the JF of the brass in the church, who died in 1523; there was the JF who had the beautiful manor house built in 1744; there was the unpopular magistrate JF who in the agricultural riots of 1830 grabbed a man in the mob, who promptly escaped by slipping out of his Dorset smock! Moreton church was also built by JF in 1776 and has been described by Newman and Pevsner as a 'gem of a Georgian Gothick building'.

The Framptons were 'improvers' particularly noted for their enthusiasm in developing the water meadows along the Frome and Piddle in the eighteenth century. A Moreton improver of another class, and perhaps typical of those who made what use they could of the heathlands, was William White. He dragged himself up from a day labourer to become a farmer of 120 acres 'by severe self-denial and the most exhausting industry'. Part of this was spent in taming 16 acres from the heath.

WALK SIX

Thomas Hardy Country

Introduction: To the west of Dorchester, which is the county town of Dorset, the river Frome winds its way to the sea in a wide valley that runs parallel to the distant coast. This ancient tributary of the Solent River is held to its course by the downs which stretch to the sea in the south and by high lands to the north. It was in this area of rather poor soils, a mixture of heath and woodland, that the great novelist-poet Thomas Hardy was born and brought up.

Despite substantial changes since his time, this country still holds the same powerful, almost mystic forces which seem to propel his characters. It is the 'Egdon Heath' depicted in *The Return of the Native:* 'The face of the heath by its mere complexion added half an hour to evening; it could in like manner retard the dawn, sadden noon, anticipate the frowning of storms scarcely generated, and intensify the opacity of a moonless midnight to a cause of shaking and dread.'

Great words, but it should also be said that the heath can be rather nice, too! The countryside that Hardy knew intimately is ideal for the walker. It offers a variety of different types of scenery in a small area and is full of memories for those who have read the author's novels, particularly *Under the Greenwood Tree.*

Distance: A circular route of about 4 miles (6½ km). It will take 2-3 hours. O.S. map, 1:50,000, Sheet 194.

Refreshments: During the summer cream teas can be had at a house near Thomas Hardy's birthplace at Higher Bockhampton. At Kingston Maurward, near Lower Bockhampton, is Yalbury Cottage Restaurant.

How to get there: There is limited car parking at the start of the walk, which is a lay-by beside a road that runs through Puddletown Forest. From the Dorchester-Bournemouth A35 road, turn south

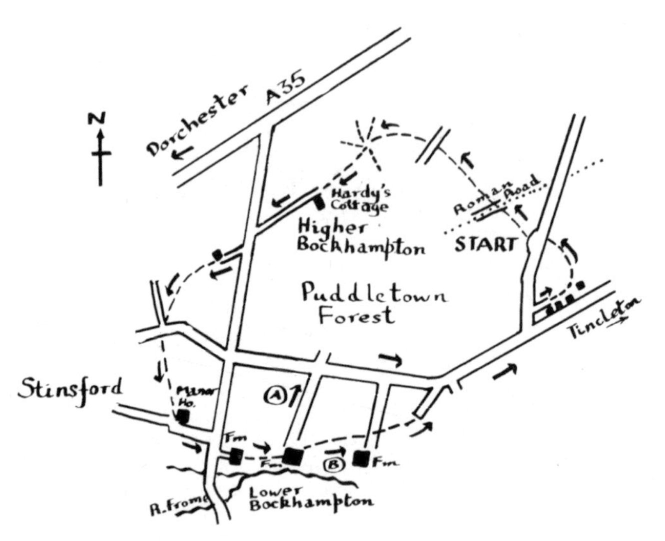

one mile east of Tolpuddle on the B3390 and pass through Affpuddle ('Tolchurch' and 'East Egdon' respectively as Hardy called them). Two miles south of Affpuddle, turn right at a cross-roads to Tincleton (Hardy: 'Stickleford') and then right two miles beyond the village, onto a road signposted to Puddletown (Hardy: Weatherbury). The lay-by where the walk starts will be found on the left-hand side after about half a mile.

The walk: The first part of the walk is within woodland and needs careful map-reading. A clear track runs from the lay-by into the forest, forking after about 200 yards. Take the right-hand arm and continue until the path is crossed by another track on the edge of open lands with trees ahead. This latter track follows the line of the Roman road between Dorchester and Salisbury. Continue across the junction, ignoring a fork to the right after about a 100 yards, but taking the left-hand arm of a second fork reached after a similar distance.

The path climbs into woodland and crosses a major track before climbing steeply alongside a series of small hillocks cum barrows on the left. At the top of the rise, six tracks meet. Ignore the track that turns sharp left and continue along the next track clockwise, making sure not to take the minor path that almost immediately leads off the latter to the left.

The track is marked with blue arrows and leads down to Higher Bockhampton and the cottage in which Thomas Hardy was born in June 1840. It is a typical thatched cottage with a garden which at the right time of year is ablaze with traditional country flowers. During the summer months the gardens of the cottage, which is owned by the National Trust, are open to view every day, but its interior can only be seen by appointment with the occupant.

Where the path meets the cottage stands a rough-hewn granite monument which records that it was in this house that Hardy wrote *Far from the Madding Crowd* and *Under the Greenwood Tree*. In the latter it was depicted as the home of Reuben Dewy, the carrier.

The walk continues down the access drive to the cottage and turns left at the road which is met after a short distance. It then turns right almost immediately along a track and passes through a gate to the left of a farm building that stands at the very end. To the left are fine views of the distant hills that, as it were, keep the river Frome flowing east.

The path enters a field: keep to the right-hand boundary and pass through a gate into a second field. Walk straight across this field towards a gate at the bottom right-hand corner, where the path meets a track running on lower ground towards a minor road. The route continues across the road to Stinsford, where Thomas Hardy was christened and his heart was buried close to other members of his family in the grave of his first wife. (His ashes were buried in Westminster Abbey.)

In the village, to the right of the path as it crosses grassland, can be seen the imposing sight of Kingston Maurward House, an early eighteenth-century house encased in dressed Portland stone, now occupied by the Dorset College of Agriculture. The path comes out at Manor Farm, which gets its name from the Old Manor House alongside, a fine building, dating from the end of the sixteenth century.

A road beside the house leads to Stinsford, which lies a short distance to the west. Called 'Mellstock' by Hardy, its church was the one whose choir provided the inspiration for *Under the Greenwood Tree*. There are still many traces of the scene described by Hardy, including the massive vases which topped the entrance to the churchyard.

The walk continues from the Old Manor House by turning left (east) along the road and then soon turning right at a T-junction with a minor road through the pretty villages of Kingston Maurward and Lower Bockhampton (Hardy: 'Lower Mellstock'). On the north west corner of the junction stands the School House, where Hardy obtained his earliest education and Fancy Day taught in *Under the Greenwood Tree*.

Hereafter, the route turns left before a bridge over an arm of the river Frome and passes through a farmyard. It runs close to the sparkling waters of the river towards a patch of woodland, which it keeps to the right.

Route A: If time is short at this point, the walk can be continued by turning left along a farm track and then right along a minor road. After a mile there is a turning off to the left to Puddletown (mentioned in the 'How to get there' section). Instructions for returning to the car park by this route continue below at *.

Route B: A more interesting, but more difficult route is to take a footpath which continues through the farmyard ahead and then takes a rough track travelling to the east. The route continues in a roughly easterly direction via a gate, across a field to a stile over a drainage ditch and so to two more stiles which cross a farm track into another field. Yet another stile will be found at the far side of this field and the path then cuts up to meet a track leading to Norris Mill Farm. The route continues along a track to the left to a minor road, where it turns right. After a few hundred yards, a turning to the left, signposted to Puddletown is reached. Instructions for returning to the car park by this route continue below:

*Almost immediately after turning left along the road to Puddletown, a bridleway leading off to the right will be seen. After 200 yards it comes to a drive to a house on the right: turn left and almost immediately take the left-hand arm of a forked track on the edge of mature woodland. The path curves round and forks again: the walk continues via the left arm (following blue arrows), and soon leads back to the lay-by where it commenced.

Historical Notes

Higher Bockhampton: ('Upper Mellstock'), near Dorchester ('Casterbridge'), is the tiny hamlet where Thomas Hardy was born in 1840 in the house built 40 years earlier by his great-grandfather. Visitors to Dorset can hardly avoid acquiring some knowledge of the life of this great man. After being articled to a firm of architects in Dorchester and living in London for five years, he returned to his home county to live at Weymouth. In 1885 he moved to Max Gate, the house on the outskirts of Dorchester which he designed and where he lived until his death in 1928. It stands a mile to the south east of the town, on the northern side of the A352. A re-creation of his study, complete with the pens with which he wrote his novels, can be seen in the County Museum, Dorchester.

Stinsford is the 'mother village' of the Bockhamptons and the other nearby settlements that do not have a church. It was here that the musicians depicted in *Under the Greenwood Tree* played their fiddles in a gallery that, like so many others, has gone. St Michael's was the Hardy family's parish church and Thomas Hardy's heart is buried in the graveyard. There is a stained glass window to his memory in the church. Cecil Day-Lewis, poet laureate and Professor of Poetry at Oxford, who was much influenced by Hardy, is also buried here.

Kingston Maurward House, which is now occupied by the Dorset College of Agriculture, stands on the east side of Stinsford. It was built in 1717-20 by George Pitt, who married Lora Grey, the last heiress of a family that had long connections with the area. There is a marble bust of him in Stinsford church, dated 1734, with the rather stuffy inscription: 'He made ample Provision for a numerous issue and rendred the Figure of his relict not unworthy of her Ancestors, whose ancient seat of Kingston in this parish he rebuilt.'

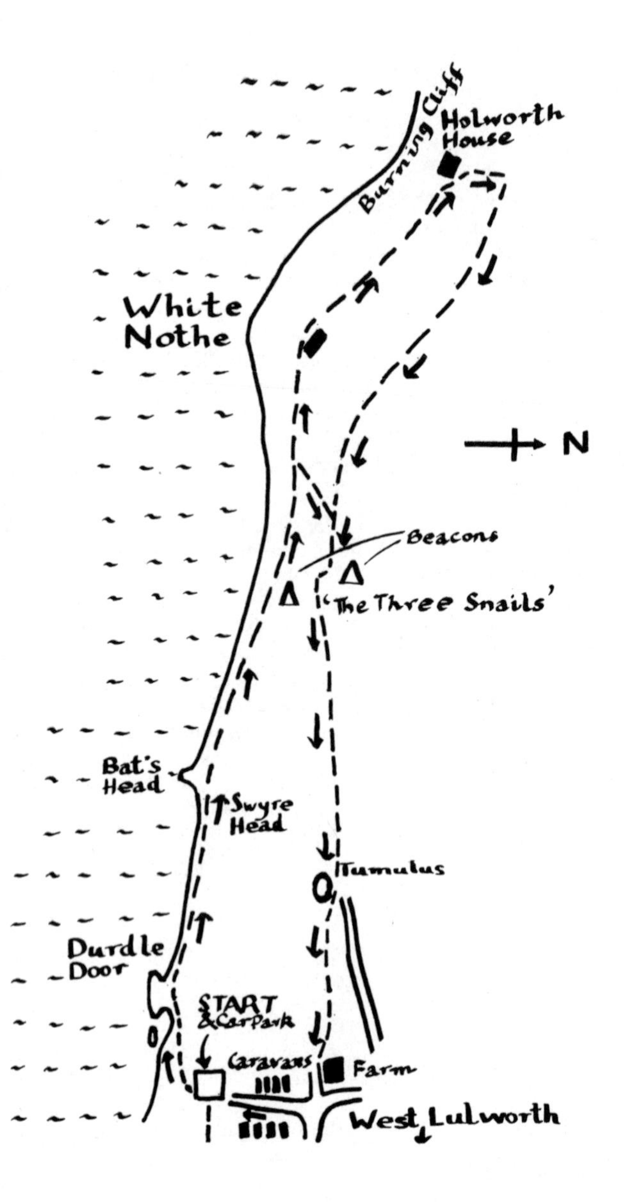

Burning Cliff
Holworth House
White Nothe
N
Beacons
'The Three Snails'
Bat's Head
Swyre Head
Tumulus
Durdle Door
START & Car Park
Caravans
Farm
West Lulworth

WALK SEVEN

Durdle Door to Burning Cliff

Introduction: This is the section of the Dorset Coast Path which includes Durdle Door, one of the Seven Wonders of Dorset. This great natural archway has been cut by the sea through a remnant of the harder limestones that are abundant further east. Although the cliffs hereabouts are generally of chalk, the coast between Mupe Bay and Dungy Head is protected by a limestone bar that peters out completely at Durdle Door. This is a continuation of the Portland and Purbeck beds, which are of course renowned for their stone. It has been breached in places, resulting in such features as Lulworth Cove and Stair Hole, which have been scooped out of the softer rocks behind.

Like much of the Dorset coast, if the walker along this stretch looks landward and tries to forget the sea, it is easy to imagine that this is North Dorset or perhaps even North Hampshire. Hence, the paths combine the pleasures of being by the sea with those of hill walking.

Distance: Route A: about 4 miles (6½ km), a circular route that can be completed in about 2 hours. Route B: 6 miles (9½ km), taking about 3 hours. O.S. map, 1:50,000, Sheet 194.

Refreshments: These are available in the summer at a kiosk in Durdle Door Camp and at several places in the village of West Lulworth, which is very popular with visitors.

How to get there: Take the A35 from Poole towards Bere Regis and Dorchester and then follow the A351 to Wareham and Wool. Take the B3071 signposted to West Lulworth at Wool Rail Station and continue past the Royal Armoured Corps Gunnery School into the delightful stone-built village. At the War Memorial take the right-hand fork and after a quarter of a mile turn right at a T-junction towards Newlands Farm. After a mile a turning to the left passes through Durdle Door Camp to a public car park on the clifftop.

The walk: From the car park a very steep well-marked path runs towards a dramatic mass of limestone which lies offshore and contains Durdle Door. Before the archway itself is reached, the way passes along the rim of the western side of Man o' War Bay, a delightful semi-circular cove protected by a broken rocky bar, where skin divers and bathers gather in the summer. The cliffs surrounding this popular sun-trap look remarkably gentle, but, as a public notice reminds: 'Cliff climbing is dangerous. It causes deaths every year.'

Beyond the bay, Durdle Door itself can be seen from the great white cliffs that stretch to Swyre Head and beyond. Durdle Door is continually being eroded by the sea and will presumably fall one day, like other stacks have done; it is therefore good to see that Bat's Hole, a small 'apprentice' archway, has already started to form in Bats Head, the rocky headland that sticks out beyond the cliffs of Swyre Head.

The walk continues by crossing one of the steepest valleys on this part of the coast. With a touch of typical Dorset humour, it is locally called Scratchy Bottom! The climb to Swyre Head is made easier by a natural staircase cut by walkers' feet.

From the top of the climb can be seen two prominent beacons, one on the skyline and another lower down to the south. The walk will pass both of these in turn, starting with the lower one. This is the sort of coastline where jackdaws gather and the peregrine falcon was once common. The route rises beyond Bat's Head, along a prominent path to the lower of the beacons mentioned. The gaunt, triangular mark is without any sort of inscription, which is a pity for such a beautiful spot.

Route A: This shorter route continues inland at a marked stile beyond the beacon: it runs at an acute angle along a field boundary to the second of the beacons (for commentary, skip to * below).

Route B: The longer route continues past a group of coastguard cottages at the top of White Nothe (said to be the highest buildings on the Dorset coast, 167 metres above sea level) and then remains a quarter of a mile from the sea for about a mile. The area on the seaward side of the path is dangerous for walking, due to extensive slippage of the limestone and Wealden rocks that overlie gault clay. The area between White Nothe and Burning Cliff has been owned by the National Trust since 1968. It was depicted as the smugglers' escape route in J. Meade Falkner's classic adventure story, *Moonfleet*. Burning Cliff takes its name from fires which raged here for several years in the 1820s. These are said to have been due to the ignition of oily bituminous rocks by iron pyrites.

Just beyond Holworth House the path turns inland and after a short distance turns right towards Daggers Gate. After a mile or so through fine rolling downland it approaches the second of the beacons already mentioned above.

*Neither Route A nor B reach the beacon, though they get close: they skirt it to the south, doglegging around a field boundary and passing a large piece of rock inscribed with the name of Llewelyn Powys, a writer who died in 1939 at the age of 45. A little further on the path passes three remarkable sculptures set in crude stone surrounds in a field bank. They are massive sculptures of snails by Peter Randall-Page.

Both routes A and B come together and continue across fields towards Durdle Door Camp, which can be seen ahead, reaching a prominent tumulus planted with a single hawthorn. Just beyond this point the path forks half-right towards Newlands Farm Camp Site. It keeps to high ground above Scratchy Bottom and soon becomes a track, which leads to Newlands Farm and the main entrance to Durdle Door Camp.

There is easy access to West Lulworth from the car park at Durdle Door Camp, via a footpath that leads off from the left-hand side (east) of the car park and runs under a prominent tumulus on Hambury Tout.

Historical Notes

The Weld Family and Lulworth: The land hereabouts is owned by the estates of the Weld family, one of the prominent families of Dorset. Their connection with the county started in 1641, when a London merchant, Humphrey Weld, bought a modest lodge at East Lulworth. This had been originally built by Lord Bindon of Bindon Castle, near Wool, in 1608 at the suggestion of the Earl of Salisbury.

The lodge was called Lulworth Castle and was extended and developed to its full glory by the Welds, who lived there until 1929 when it was gutted by fire. The gaunt ruins are as close to being a fairy-tale castle as any in Dorset and still stand.

In the grounds of the castle are Anglican and Roman Catholic churches. The latter was permitted to Thomas Weld in the 1780s by the special dispensation of George III at a time when Roman Catholics were still widely persecuted. The only stipulation the monarch made was that the chapel should not look like one, which explains its rather strange shape, more like an astronomical observatory than a house of worship.

West Lulworth: This is the popular village that stands beside Lulworth Cove, a marvellously rounded bay that has been cut out of soft rock as if by some giant ice-cream scoop. 'Each wave spreads out into a widening circle as it nears the beach, so that the water viewed from the heights is rippled by concentric rings like the lid of a flat sea shell', wrote Sir Frederick Treves with the precision expected of a surgeon in his *Highways and Byways in Dorset*.

Lulworth is famed for its fossil forest, which lies to the east of the bay.

Ringstead and Holworth: Ringstead village to the west of Burning Cliff survived as a settlement until the fifteenth century. Traces of streets and ruined buildings can still be found close to Glebe Cottage, which incorporates in its structure the chancel arch of the church. Ringstead, which is now owned by the National Trust, appears in the Domesday Book. It seems that there were two hamlets, East and West Ringstead, and like other isolated settlements beside the sea they became vulnerable to piracy. Holworth House, which stands a mile to the east, is another example of a 'deserted' hamlet, now reduced to a single house.

Llewelyn Powys, whose memorial stands beside the walk, was one of a remarkable trio of literary brothers from Dorchester. The best-known of them was John Cowper Powys, whose *Glastonbury Romance* has had a cult following.

Llewelyn Powys was extremely fond of walking and wrote a large number of articles and stories. One of his last books was *Dorset Essays* published in 1935.

Hambury Tout and Newlands Warren: There are a large number of prehistoric relics in the area around Durdle Door Camp. These include the bell barrow on Hambury Tout (tout: meaning a lookout), which stands immediately to the east of the car park. This was found to contain the remains of a skeleton when it was opened at the remarkably early date of 1790. The body had been buried in a crouched position and may have been provided with a pot of food, presumably in the belief that this would assist in reaching the after-life.

Newlands Warren, which stretches landward of Swyre Head and White Nothe, hold the remains of an extensive area of Celtic fields, covering about 850 acres.

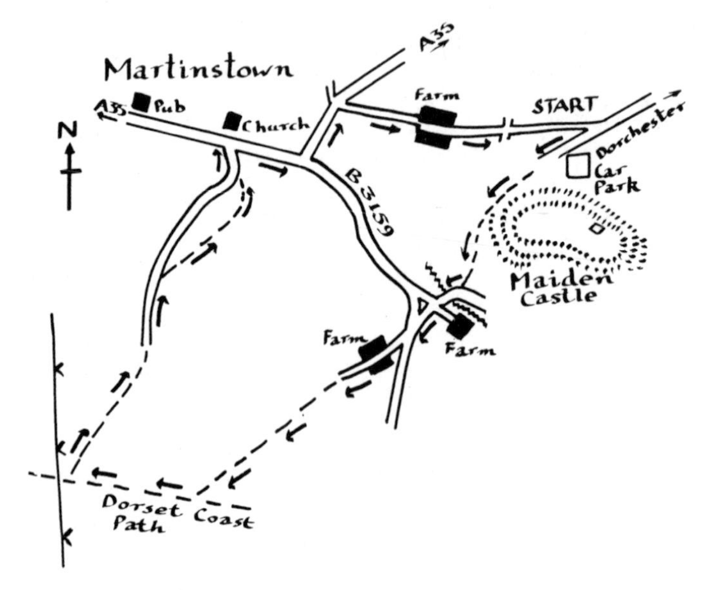
Martinstown
A35
Pub
Church
N
A35
Farm
START
Dorchester
Car Park
B3159
Maiden Castle
Farm
Farm
Dorset Coast Path

WALK EIGHT

Maiden Castle

Introduction: The capital cities of many counties have endured in more or less the same place for centuries, if not millennia. But in some cases, important centres founded on hilltops in the Iron Age were beseiged by Roman troops and later refounded in the valleys. Thus hill climbers may find themselves visiting deserted sites that once hummed with activity. Salisbury has Old Sarum, Winchester has St Catherine's Hill and Dorchester has Maiden Castle, which is the most impressive of the three.

Great earthworks like Maiden Castle inevitably set thoughts racing. The naturalist-writer W.H. Hudson captured the feelings that most of us must have experienced as he sat on a barrow in the New Forest. He felt a kinship with the 'long, long dead', though modern archaeologists might not agree with his comment that they were 'men who knew not life in towns'. He confessed: 'I sat there for hours, held by the silence and solitariness of that mound of the ancient dead.'

This walk passes within sight of Portland Bill and the working harbour at Weymouth, which serves its dignified capital at Dorchester. Maiden Castle was served by earlier ports, where the Veneti and other tribes from Brittany landed, bringing their more advanced cultures to a British 'backwater'.

Distance: A circular walk of about 4 miles (6½km) with only moderate slopes, taking about 2 hours, plus the time chosen to explore Maiden Castle. O.S. map, 1:50,000, Sheet 194.

Refreshments: The Brewers Arms at the west end of the main street of Martinstown advertises 'real ale and real food'.

How to get there: From Dorchester, take the A354 towards Weymouth and turn right just outside the town centre, into Maiden Castle Road. There is a car park immediately underneath the great earthwork, but for the purposes of this walk a slightly better place to park is a few hundred yards before the car park, on the verge, where a track forks off to the right.

The walk: From the car park a track runs up to the fortified western entrance of the hill fort, which was protected by a 'maze' of banks. A detailed exploration of the site gives superb views in all directions and takes about an hour (the perimeter is about a mile round). The first camp was set up in Neolithic times on the eastern part of the site. During the Iron Age the original site was extended to the west and fortified with a succession of ditches and banks.

A small gate near the western entrance leads to a track which runs south between the old fort and Hog Hill. It leads downhill towards a farmhouse, where it meets a minor road. Here the route turns right onto the road, which soon passes over the South Winterbourne, a small tributary of the river Frome. At a fork, take the left-hand limb and after 100 yards turn left at a T-junction and almost immediately right along the driveway of Higher Ashton Farm. This is the start of a bridleway signposted to Ridge Hill.

The path continues through the farmyard along a concrete road that passes into a field with a small tumulus to the left and a steep dry valley to the right. The view of Maiden Castle behind is good justification of that habit that the walker should acquire of 'looking back'.

Blue arrows help to keep to the bridleway, which cuts up to a gate at the top left-hand corner of the field. The path proceeds to a 'telegraph' pole a short distance ahead, where it turns right into a field, towards a patch of woodland. It skirts a group of tumuli to the left of the wood and runs to another gate beside a depot at the top left-hand corner of the field. Here the route turns left and climbs to a ridge marked with a dry-stone wall. This is Ridge Hill, along which runs a stretch of the alternative, inland route of the Dorset Coast Path. This was prescribed to avoid the built-up areas of Weymouth, whose northerly bounds nonetheless stretch to this isolated downland.

All along this part of the walk, which follows an ancient coastal ridgeway, there are sites of burial mounds, but the ridge itself seems to have been the most favoured site. Perhaps it was something to do with the superb views of the coast which you can see from here. The great mass of Portland Bill stretches out beyond Portland Harbour and Weymouth Bay, defying the encroaching waters with its harder rocks.

The path continues to the right, towards the distant escarpment of Bronkham Hill with the Hardy Monument beyond (erected to honour Nelson's captain, not the novelist). The view is marred by three lines of pylons, but they have their uses: in the shadow of the first line the route turns right, signposted to Martinstown. The path passes to the left of yet more tumuli and it can be seen snaking ahead in the bottom of a valley.

Just beyond the third tumulus the path leads through a gate and down to the valley bottom, where it continues along a farm track. After about a quarter of a mile, just before the track makes uphill past an old chalk working, the path forks off to the right. It continues along a field boundary on the left towards a prominent tumulus at Clandon, a mile away. After a few hundred yards it passes through a gate and goes uphill along a track. At the top of the rise, it meets a private metalled road with the tower of Martinstown church ahead.

Martinstown alias Winterbourne St Martin is a beautiful stone-built village. The path crosses the brook that runs down one side of the main street and comes out opposite the church. At the west end of the village is the local pub, the Brewers Arms.

The walk turns right (east) along the main street and then left at a T-junction, signposted to Dorchester. For a quarter of a mile it keeps to this road, which can be rather busy – so *take care*. On a bend, a footpath forks off to the right, opposite a minor road, and leads to the hamlet of Clandon, where it meets a track. The route continues straight ahead through the yard, past The Paddocks, a modern house built in 1982. Ahead is Dorchester and the starting point of the walk alongside Maiden Castle. There is a good view of the old earthwork that recalls the words of Thomas Hardy: 'At one's every step forward it rises higher against the south sky, with an obtrusive personality that compels the senses to regard it and consider.'

Historical Notes

Maiden Castle was originally excavated by the extrovert archaeologist Sir Mortimer Wheeler in the 1930s. It was at a time when the idea that hill forts were merely places of refuge was being modified. It was being realised that some of these bleak hill sites once contained small townships and that Maiden Castle was probably one of them.

Sir Mortimer's excavations established that there were several distinct phases to the history of Maiden Castle. First, the eastern end was occupied by a Neolithic (Late Stone Age) village during 3000-2000 BC. With the exception of its use for a huge Neolithic bank burial, it was then deserted for about 1500 years. Then followed several stages of Iron Age occupation, culminating in the four-fold (and in some places seven-fold) ramparts that now encircle the entire hill. Finally, a few decades after its overthrow by Roman troops in about 43 AD, it became deserted once more. But it was not ignored: a lone pagan temple was erected in about 380 AD at the eastern end, where its foundations can still be traced, and at least one Saxon was buried there.

Looking in detail at the findings of Sir Mortimer, which are fully displayed in Dorchester's County Museum, the Neolithic village covered an area of 10-15 acres and was occupied by people whose culture probably originated from across the Channel, in Brittany. This was an ongoing source of influence which often determined the fates of Maiden Castle in succeeding eras. The most interesting find from the Neolithic site was an idol crudely carved in chalk, which was probably linked with a mother-goddess cult originating from the Continent.

The later Neolithic burial site is especially interesting as the largest known example of a bank barrow. Although it cannot now be seen on the surface, excavation showed that it extended along the centre of the hill for 537 metres (587 yards). At the eastern end was found a ritual burial, later than the main bank, of the body of a man who had been hacked to pieces.

Complete desertion of the hill after about 1500 BC (with the exception of a Bronze Age hunter who lost his spear!) was probably the result of a deteriorating climate, but in about 500 BC the site started to be reoccupied. This was originally only at the eastern end used by the Neolithic settlement, but later the rest of the hill top was occupied and defended in the way that can be seen today. The first Iron Age people at Maiden Castle stored their corn in deep pits cut into the chalk, protected by a single defence bank about two metres high. This was originally supported by a timber palisade, which later was replaced by the sort of dry-stone wall that is still commonplace hereabouts. Sir Mortimer has described the life as that of a 'self-sufficient, unenterprising peasantry'.

The later Iron Age phases of Maiden Castle, which occupied the whole hill, were the result of a 'bow wave' of migrating Celtic peoples 'moved on' by Roman occupation of Gaul. It is possible that part of the Veneti tribe, after being displaced from its homelands in southern Brittany, came to Maiden Castle and developed it to its full potential. The complex defence works have been described as an antidote for the sling, the weapon that seems to have dominated military thinking from about the second century BC. A cache of 20,000 beach pebbles suitable for slinging 100 yards was discovered at Maiden Castle. On the eve of the Roman onslaught of the hill it was an important centre (perhaps the capital) of the area occupied by the Durotriges, who lent their name to *Durnovaria*, the Roman town which grew up on the site of present-day Dorchester.

Maiden Castle fell to the Second Augustan Legion under the command of a future emperor, Vespasian. He breached the ramparts one by one at the eastern end and then set fire to huts and stormed the eastern gateway under cover of smoke. A gruesome relic of the early stages of the battle is the skeleton of a man with his spine pierced by a ballista, one of the heavy arrows used by Roman artillery. Excavations have revealed the graves of many of the Durotrigians slaughtered at the time, who nonetheless were buried with the usual tributes of drink and food.

Martinstown: As in many places, the key to this delightful Dorset village lies in its church. Dating from the early twelfth century, it was rebuilt in the perpendicular style towards the end of the fourteenth century and 'restored' in the early years of the present century. It has a lovely tower, a fine timbered roof and a huge chancel arch. The chancel itself 'nods' to the north-east, perhaps in deference to the fallen head of Christ on the cross. There is an early twelfth century font in Purbeck marble.

The village takes its name from the chantry of St Martin, which was founded here in 1367, probably in the north aisle. Prayers for the souls of the dead were said by a priest, who lived opposite (not in the house which is now there, The Chantry!). The alternative name for the village, Winterbourne St Martin, derives from the intermittent nature of the stream which runs alongside its main street.

One memory of a long tradition which was until 1983 kept alive in the village is Martinstown Fair, originally granted by Henry III in 1268. It was held on St Martin's Day, November 11th, and combined the serious business of selling livestock with a lot of fun.

WALK NINE

Chesil Beach and The Mohuns of Fleet

Introduction: This part of the Dorset coast is completely dominated by Chesil Beach, the 16-mile long bank of pebbles which stretches from Abbotsbury to Portland Bill. It is internationally unique and a great example of the eastward drift of materials that happens all along the south coast. The resulting spits are usually quite short, but in the case of Chesil the flint and quartzite pebbles that start their journey at Abottsbury soon get involved in an immense 'traffic jam'. This is caused by the great mass of Portland acting as a huge groyne and preventing the pebbles from moving on.

The net effect of Chesil Beach, acting as a reef 200 hundred yards wide, is to protect the coast behind it from erosion. Unlike the Dorset coast to the east, the shore here is without cliffs and runs alongside the gentle Fleet Water, which is impounded behind the bank. The contrast between the raging seas of White Nothe and Swyre Head and the creek-like shores of the East Fleet could hardly be greater!

Distance: This walk covers about 5½ miles (9km) over terrain with quite gentle slopes. It follows a circular route and should take about 2 hours.

Refreshments: The Moonfleet Hotel is open to non-residents, and the Elm Tree Inn is an excellent Devenish pub near Langton Herring church.

How to get there: From Dorchester, take the A354 towards Weymouth. Beyond Upwey, five miles to the south, turn right into Nottington Lane, signposted to Nottington, Chickerell and Abbotsbury. Turn left at a T-junction in Nottington, signposted to

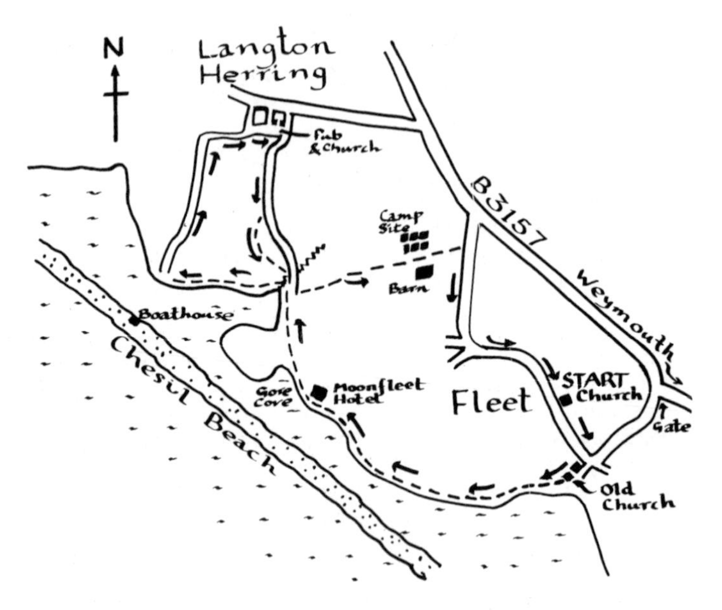

Chickerell and follow a rather tortuous road through Coldharbour. At a primary school, turn right into East Street and follow the road through Chickerell village until it meets the B3157 Weymouth-Abbotsbury road. Turn right and after a quarter of a mile turn left at a roundabout, signposted to Fleet. (A longer route with less chance of getting lost is to follow the A354 into Weymouth and then pick up the B3157.)

Follow the Fleet turning to the shore, where it bends to the right and passes Holy Trinity Church on the right. The church encourages visitors to park in its driveway, for a small donation.

The walk: If you do not already know of the connection between the village of Fleet and the children's classic *Moonfleet*, you will soon learn all about it!

Walking in the Fleet area will soon make you realise that Meade Falkner could hardly have chosen a better location for his book; he was fortunate to know the area (his father served at Wyke Regis church) and to grasp the opportunity to write a great story.

Before setting off, look in the porch of Holy Trinity church, where a tablet tells how it was built at the expense of George Gould, the rector, after the old church had been ruined by a great storm which swept over Chesil Beach in November 1824. According to reported eye-witness accounts, the water 'came up as fast as a horse could gallop' and reached a depth of 30 feet. It smashed the nave of the church and several cottages. The chancel still stands, and is of particular interest for the brasses of two members of the Mohun family which it still contains. These show a family of five boys and eight girls, but in fact it is known that the mother, Margaret Mohun, bore a total of 17 children, some of whom presumably did not survive.

To reach the old church and the start of the walk, turn left out of Holy Trinity and after several hundred yards turn right along a signposted path. The old churchyard is immediately alongside the row of cottages ahead. Under the chancel is the Mohun vault, a vital element in the *Moonfleet* adventure, though descriptions of the church more closely fit Meade Falkner's father's church at Wyke Regis.

The footpath continues to the edge of Fleet Water with the great mass of Chesil Beach almost a mile away. To the left can be seen the entrance to the lagoon and beyond the high land of Portland Bill, known to sailors as 'The Snout'. The east end of the Fleet Water is tidal and salty, but to the west it progressively becomes brackish and unmoving.

Chesil and the Fleet are recognised areas of international importance for their wildlife. Many sea birds breed on the beach and for that reason it is 'out of bounds' to visitors during the summer. Similarly, such sports as fishing and boating are generally prohibited on Fleet Water, which has had some form of protection since the end of the fourteenth century. It is said to be the second oldest nature reserve in the country (excluding hunting reserves) and was particularly protected for its mute swans, which are still abundant at the well-known swannery and bird reserve at Abbotsbury.

The footpath runs west from Fleet and keeps to the shore all the way to the top of a small bay called Gore Cove. It passes to the south of the former manor house owned by the Mohuns, which is now run as the Moonfleet Hotel. The route cuts across the peninsula of Herbury and then turns left on a signposted path across a small wooden bridge. It continues alongside the Fleet

Water for half a mile and then turns right along a track, opposite a prominent boathouse that stands on the Chesil shore.

As the track is mounted, lovely views unfold inland, and the distant Hardy Monument (honouring Nelson's captain, not the writer) can be seen. The track turns sharp right and then left into the quiet stone-built village of Langton Herring. Within a short distance, the road forks: the church and Elm Tree Inn, a fine pub, will be found along the right-hand limb of the fork.

The walk continues by turning back towards the Fleet by a track that runs to the south. With the pub entrance at your back, turn right along a cul-de-sac, past a Methodist chapel on the left and turn left in front of Fleet Way Cottage onto a track. After a quarter of a mile it meets a strip of woodland: the route continues either along the track or via a footpath that skirts the wood to the right. Either way the path returns to the Fleet Water at a point passed earlier to the north of Herbury. After a short distance the route turns left uphill, signposted to Bagwell. The path goes straight on for a mile or so, keeping to the left-hand edge of farmland. It passes to the left of a lovely old barn at Bagwell Farm and into a campsite complete with telephone and shop (in season).

Beside a children's playground at the entrance to the site, the path crosses a stile onto a track, which it follows to the right, passing the entrance to West Fleet Holiday Farm. At a crossroads it meets a quiet metalled road, which leads to the left to Holy Trinity church and the car park.

Historical Notes

Fleet shares that fate of so many other villages by the sea: it was once on the main road but engineers later decided to re-route the highway some distance inland. The old road between Weymouth and Bridport passed through Wyke Regis and across to East Fleet via what is now a footpath cum track. It continued past the old church at Fleet and then via Sea Barn Farm to Langton Herring, approaching via the track which forms part of this walk.

The stories of the great storms which have often devastated this part of the coastline must have been sufficient reason to reposition the road. When Fleet suffered in the notable storm of 23rd November 1824, the local people were fortunate to have a caring clergyman, whose actions are recorded in a contemporary newspaper report:

> The Reverend George Gould, Rector of Fleet, a village destroyed by the late storm, intends building a new village; and with a degree of philanthropy that will ever immmortalise his name, has taken and provided for all the sufferers under his roof.

In addition to ruining the church, the storm also destroyed two cottages in the village, whose aged occupants had to be rescued from upstairs windows. It scattered hayricks and washed fishing boats far from their moorings. The sloop *Ebenezer* was flung up onto Chesil Beach like a toy boat.

The new church, which was dedicated five years after the disaster, was partly built as a memorial to John Gould, the rector's elder brother, whose death in 1818 had brought the Mohun/Gould fortunes to the bachelor cleric. A monument depicts John supporting a mourning young woman, presumably his widow.

There is a footnote to the destruction of the old site of the village of Fleet which seems not to have been remembered locally, namely that in 1938 five of the six cottages spared by the great storm were destroyed by fire.

The story of the Mohuns and the Goulds of Fleet would probably have long ago been forgotten if Meade Falkner had not set his story in the village. It is fairly complicated, but it boils down to about two hundred years of Mohuns holding the estate, followed by a marriage which transferred ownership to the Goulds, whose descendants (not all called Gould) held it for another 150 years or so, until 1897, the year before the publication of *Moonfleet*. When the reading public was given Meade Falkner's story it was therefore learning of distant history and there was no chance of offending a sitting squire, or of troubling him with prying tourists!

There were plenty of incidents of smuggling in the Fleet area to provide the author with raw material. Between 1800 and 1821 a total of 69 men and women were imprisoned at Dorchester for evading customs, all of them from along The Fleet and two from Fleet itself. An official report of 1831 estimated that in the country as a whole £800,000 was lost as result of smuggling, most of it from illegal imports of brandy.

Chesil Beach and The Fleet must surely rank as another of the Seven Wonders of Dorset. The stones of the beach come from a variety of sources, some from as far away as Cornwall and others from the terrace gravels of an extinct river that once flowed along the Fleet valley. They have all been mixed up by the tides, but one feature is said to enable local fishermen to determine their position, namely, that the stones are closely graded in a steady progression of size from the sands of Abbotsbury to the boulders of Portland. Also it is just possible to imagine that the sound of the waves is an aid to navigation, for 'the note of the beach varies in its course, changing from the whisper of sand to the hissing of shingle and then to the hollow rattling and rumbling of down-dragged pebbles', as Sir Frederick Treves wrote.

The Fleet is contained by Chesil Beach and takes its name from the Saxon for an inlet. It is normally a quiet, smooth area of water frequented by sea birds and the few local fishermen who are allowed to take mullet and bass from its waters. Their huts stand on the great shingle bank like relics from the past.

Langton Herring takes its name from its shape 'long town' and the family name of one of its medieval owners, Harang. The church dates from the end of the thirteenth century but was substantially enlarged and rebuilt in the early years of the last century. The vestry contains an interesting Royal Ordinance to give thanks for the harvest in 1847, which followed a sucession of poor harvests at about the time of the potato famine in Ireland.

In the last war The Fleet was used by Barnes (later Sir Barnes) Wallis to test the ideal specification for the 'bouncing bombs' used by 'the dambusters'. On the shore at Langton Herring is said to be one of the confections of steel and concrete which he used to make tests. There are no war memorials in the village for the happy reason that no one in the village was killed in either of the World Wars.

Hidden in trees alongside the B3157 to the east of the village stands Langton Cross, probably dating from the fourteenth century and used by pilgrims on their way to the monastery at Abbotsbury.

The Golden Cap Estate

Introduction: Between Bridport and the western borders of Dorset is one of the finest stretches of the county's coastline. The National Trust has long recognised its outstanding beauty and now owns more than six miles of the coast between Eype and Lyme Regis, much of it acquired in the last twenty years. The centre of this huge estate is Golden Cap, the highest cliff in southern England. Part of it was first convenanted to the National Trust by a member of the Weld family in 1936. It takes its name from the colour of its sandstone cap (which geologists confusingly call greensand, after its colour in Wealden deposits).

The coastline of the Golden Cap Estate provides a very varied terrain for the walker. There are low cliffs with 'slumping' lands falling down to the sea, wooded hills, the great cliffs of Golden Cap itself and Stonebarrow Hill above fossil-rich Cains Folly. Several areas are managed as nature reserves in association with the Dorset Naturalists' Trust, whilst some of the picturesque farms are run without the use of agricultural sprays in order to preserve 'botanically rich' grasslands.

Distance: Circular walk of about 5½ miles (9km) with a few steep climbs, but much of it on the flat. It should take about 2½ hours. As described, it starts at a relatively small car park at Langdon Wood, but could be walked from a larger parking place on Stonebarow Hill (see map). O.S. map, 1:50,000. Sheet 193.

Refreshments: The Ship Inn, Morecombelake, serves snacks, whilst a short distance to the west is Moore's Dorset Shop.

How to get there: The start is reached via the A35 from Bridport. After passing through the delightful village of Chideock, which is something of a 'tourist trap', the road climbs quite steeply. After about half a mile there is a small turning to the left along a metalled

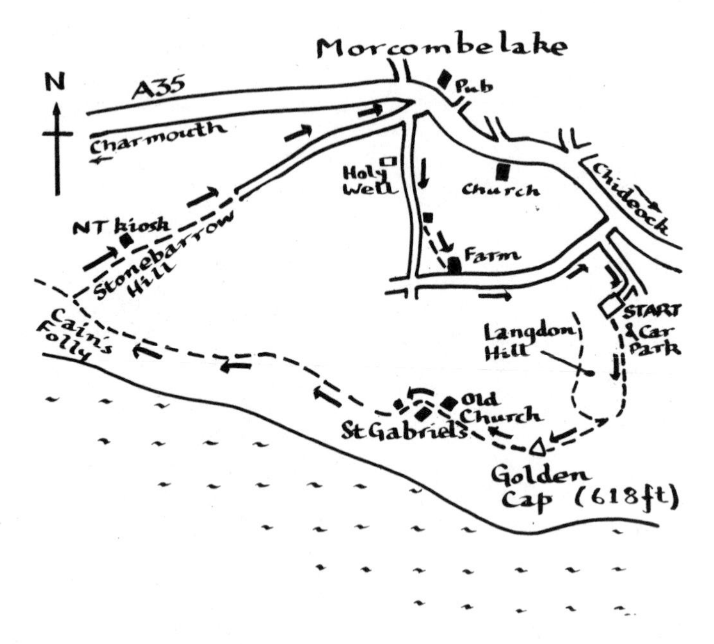

road: it is not signposted but is easily found by watching carefully for a stretch of dual carriageway that starts a few yards beyond it. After a short distance along the turning a potholed track turns off to the left and leads to the National Trust car park at Langdon Hill.

The walk: The route starts along a track which runs from a stile on the southern side of the car park, signposted to Golden Cap. To the left is a superb view of the village of Chideock, whilst ahead are glimpses of the sea. The route curves around the edge of woodland and after a fairly sharp right-hander continues down a small footpath which runs into pine woods on the left. (The track itself continues to a viewpoint, and in fact encircles the top of the hill.)

At the foot of the wood the path turns right towards Golden Cap, which is ahead. The path to the top of this great cliff, which is 618 feet high, worms its way up in a remarkably gentle way, with lovely views providing plenty of excuses to stop! At the top, which is surprisingly flat, stands an Ordnance Survey triangulation point, to the west of which is a stone erected in memory of the Earl of Antrim. During his period as chairman of the National Trust between 1966 and his death in 1977 he presided over the acquisition of much of the Golden Cap Estate.

On a clear day the view from the top of the Golden Cap extends from Portland Bill in the east to Start Point and Devon in the west. The famous Cobb at Lyme Regis, near which the Duke of Monmouth landed at the start of his futile rebellion of 1685, is clearly visible. Due north can be seen the heights of Pilsdon Pen, which at more than 900 feet above sea level is the highest point in Dorset. Immediately below is the near-deserted village of Stanton St Gabriel, which now only consists of a few holiday cottages and a ruined church. The footpath continues down to the old church, keeps to the right of the cottages and then passes through a gate to rejoin the coast path.

The route continues along the coast beside low, sandy cliffs that slump towards the sea. This is a continual hazard of the sort of geological formation found hereabouts.

Ahead are the exposed beds of the truncated end of Stonebarrow Hill, called Cains Folly: our route climbs steeply to the summit of the hill and then turns inland towards another National Trust car park, where the familiar oak-leaf flag may indicate that the trust's information centre (housed in an old radar station) is in business.

A track along the ridge of Stonebarrow Hill continues for about a mile to Morcombelake, which is seen spread out on the facing hillside as the path curves down towards the A35. The track becomes a metalled road and emerges opposite a convenient pub, the Ship Inn. A short distance along the main road to the right, on the south side, stand the premises of Moores, 'Visitors Welcome', the biscuit bakers renowned for their Dorset Knobs.

Returning to the track opposite the pub, the way back to the Langdon Hill is via a track that turns off left (due south) from the track and follows another track signposted to Golden Cap and St Wite's Well. The holy well will be found a short distance along the track on the right: it is said to have 'curative properties' for eye problems and is probably linked to the thirteenth century shrine of St Wite in the church of Whitchurch Canonicorum nearby.

The route continues towards Pickaxe Cross, but just below a house named 'Coldharbour' a footpath forks off to the left and makes its way down to the west side of Norchard Farm, whose brightly painted buildings are in marked contrast to the bracken and turf of Golden Cap and dark woods of Langdon Hill. The minor road in front of the farm is a continuation of the one turned into from the A35 at the start of the walk. To the left it runs between deep-cut banks to the potholed track that turns off to the right and returns to the car park.

Historical Notes

The Golden Cap Coastline is part of an extremely important exposure of the rocks which lie under the limestones of Portland and Purbeck. They belong to the Lias strata of the Jurassic era and were laid down in shallow seas and are older than chalk and its associated rocks of gault clay and greensand. The Lias beds run in a north easterly direction in a great band through England, through Somerset and Gloucestershire to the Yorkshire coast between the Tees and Filey Bay.

The area first acquired its reputation with fossil-hunters when in 1811 a 10-year-old girl, Mary Anning, discovered the previously unknown skeleton of an ichthyosaurus (a fish cum lizard) in the cliffs of Black Ven, between Charmouth and Lyme Regis. It took her ten years to reveal the entire 25-foot skeleton, which she later sold to the Natural History Museum, South Kensington (where it can still be seen), for a mere £23. She was the daughter of the owner of a curiosity shop and her discovery gave her the fame that is now reserved for pop singers. There is a stained glass window to her memory in the church at Lyme Regis, (akin to those found on the Continent for those who witness miracles). The town's prosperity in the last century owed much to this young girl's chance discovery and persistent chipping.

Golden Cap itself is a great knob of upper greensand and gault, though as mentioned above, the 'greensand' is in Dorset a bright gold colour. At the foot of the cliff are green ammonite beds, called after those amazing spiral fossils which show such variations within the Jurassic era.

Further west, at Cains Folly under Stonebarrow Hill, the 'golden cap' is much thinner, the ammonite beds occupy a higher position and the bottom of the cliffs expose the next layer in the Lias series, namely, the belemnite marls. As the name suggests, these rocks are rich in pencil-like belemnites, which are the fossil remains of the hard parts of cuttlefish.

Stanton St Gabriel was reduced from being a substantial community to its present condition – a ruined church and a row of cottages – over a long period. Better roads probably threatened the existence of such a small fishing village, but coastal erosion must also have contributed. Further west, at Lyme Regis, land slippage has been a perpetual problem and the tendency of its church to fall into the sea has given it a unique topsy-turvy character.

In the middle of the seventeenth century there were no less than 23 families living in Stanton St Gabriel, but within a hundred years this had declined drastically. Then in 1825 the complete extinction of the village was virtually made certain when the main route between Bridport and Exeter, which had formerly passed through St Gabriel, was rerouted via Morecombelake, two miles inland.

The few houses that remain at the old site are now let to holidaymakers, whilst the only substantial relics of the church to remain are a south door, which is remarkably low, and part of the west wall containing a fragment of window surround.

Morecombelake took over where Stanton St Gabriel left off. In 1841 its church, dedicated to St Gabriel, was built and is said to incorporate a rood beam taken from the old church by the sea.

Morecombelake is today best known for the Dorset Knob biscuits made there by Moores, bakers in the village since 1880. These confections of dough, butter and sugar were originally made elsewhere on the family farm as a way of using up odd bits of dough after the bread had been baked. The Dorset Knobs were baked in the dying heat of the oven and probably got their name from their resemblance to a type of button made in the county. Three slow bakings over 8-10 hours are needed to make the biscuits, which for business reasons are only produced between January and March. Dorset Ginger biscuits and Walnut Crunches are also made in the Morecombelake bakery, which is open to visitors and turns out 50,000 biscuits per day!

Further reading

Ashley, H., *Explore Dorset*, 1985
Ashley, H., *Dorset: A Portrait in Colour*, 1986
Bettey, J.H., *Dorset, (City & County Histories)*, 1974
Cullingford, C.N., *A History of Dorset*, 1980
Edwards, A.M., *Discovering Hardy's Wessex, 2nd Ed.*, 1982
Gant, R., *Dorset Villages*, 1980
Holland, C., *Thomas Hardy's Wessex Scene*, 1948
Hyams, J., *Dorset*, 1970
Jackman, B., *Dorset Coast Path*, 1979
Legg, R., *Purbeck Island,*, 1972
Mee, A., *Dorset, (The Kings England)*, 1967
Newman, J. & Pevsner, N., *Dorset, (The Buildings of England)*, 1972
Taylor, C., *Dorset, (The Making of the English Landscape)*, 1970
Treves, Sir F., *Highways & Byways in Dorset*, 1906